I0017492

Preventing Ransomware:
A Practical Guide for Everyone

CHATGPT4o with j. p. ames

Introduction

As a 40-year computer scientist, I thought it could be useful to guide everyone to a solution to preventing the scourge of ransomware.

Ransomware can hit anyone, anywhere if protection systems are not in place.

This is a practical guide anyone can use to prevent ransomware.

MY friend HAL (CHATGPT4o) wrote this book, with me as advisor.

Summary: Preventing Ransomware: A Practical Guide for Everyone

In today's digital age, ransomware poses a significant threat to businesses of all sizes. "Preventing Ransomware: A Practical Guide for Everyone" is an essential resource for small business owners, IT professionals, and anyone looking to protect their digital assets from malicious attacks.

This comprehensive guide covers everything you need to know about ransomware, from understanding how it works to implementing effective defenses. You'll learn how to conduct thorough risk assessments, create robust incident response plans, and deploy the latest security tools and practices to keep your business safe.

Inside this book, you will find:

- **Clear Explanations:** Understand the different types of ransomware and how they operate.
- **Step-by-Step Guides:** Learn practical steps to secure your network, systems, and data.
- **Real-World Case Studies:** Gain insights from actual ransomware incidents and how businesses overcame them.
- **Expert Advice:** Discover the best tools and strategies for preventing and responding to attacks.
- **Actionable Checklists:** Ensure you have covered all bases with easy-to-follow checklists and templates.

Whether you're a small business owner, a manager, or an IT specialist, this book equips you with the knowledge and tools needed to prevent ransomware and safeguard your business. Stay one step ahead of cybercriminals and protect your digital world with "Preventing Ransomware: A Practical Guide for Everyone."

About the Author:

Jim and HAL have combined their expertise in cybersecurity and practical experience to create a guide that is both informative and easy to understand. With a passion for helping small businesses and a deep understanding of digital threats, they bring you a book that is both timely and essential.

Table of Contents

Introduction to Cybersecurity

The Importance of Cybersecurity

In today's world, keeping your business safe from cyber threats is very important. Small businesses often think they are too small to be targeted, but attackers know that small businesses might have weaker defenses. A single ransomware attack can cause big financial losses, stop your operations, and harm your reputation.

Key Points:

- Cyberattacks can lead to downtime, loss of customer trust, and potential legal problems.
- Investing in cybersecurity is an investment in your business's future.
- Being prepared can save money compared to dealing with an attack's aftermath.

The Threat of Ransomware: An Overview

Ransomware is a type of malware that can lock you out of your systems or encrypt your files until you pay a ransom. This book will give you the knowledge and tools to protect your business from these threats, respond effectively if attacked, and recover quickly.

Key Points:

- Ransomware can make your important data unusable until you pay a ransom.
- The cost of a ransomware attack includes not only the ransom but also downtime and recovery costs.
- Understanding ransomware and having strong defenses is crucial.

Understanding Ransomware

What is Ransomware?

Ransomware is malicious software that locks your files or system and demands payment to unlock them. Attackers usually ask for payment in cryptocurrencies like Bitcoin because it's hard to trace.

Specific Details:

- **Encryption Techniques:** Ransomware uses strong encryption methods to lock your files.
- **Delivery Methods:** Common ways ransomware enters your system include phishing emails, malicious websites, and software vulnerabilities.

How Ransomware Works

Understanding how ransomware operates helps you defend against it. Here's a typical ransomware attack sequence:

1. **Infection:**

   - **Phishing Emails:** Attackers send fake emails that look real but contain malicious links or attachments.
   - **Malicious Websites:** Victims visit compromised websites that install ransomware.
   - **Software Vulnerabilities:** Attackers exploit unpatched software to gain access.

2. **Execution:**

   - The ransomware encrypts files, often starting with the most critical data.
   - Some ransomware tries to delete or encrypt backups too.

3. **Notification:**

   - The victim sees a ransom note with payment instructions.
   - The ransom amount varies, and attackers set a deadline for payment.

4. **Payment:**

   - Victims are asked to pay in cryptocurrency. However, paying doesn't guarantee data recovery and encourages more attacks.

5. **Decryption:**

   - If the ransom is paid, attackers might provide a decryption key, but it's not guaranteed.

Specific Example:

- **WannaCry Ransomware:** Spread rapidly by exploiting a Windows vulnerability, encrypting files and demanding Bitcoin ransom.

Types of Ransomware Attacks

Knowing different types of ransomware helps tailor your defenses:

1. **Crypto Ransomware:**

   - **Example:** CryptoLocker encrypts files and demands payment.
   - **Defense:** Regular backups, anti-virus software, and email filtering.

2. **Locker Ransomware:**

   - **Example:** Reveton locks you out of your system and shows a fake law enforcement warning.
   - **Defense:** Strong password policies and secure access controls.

3. **Scareware:**

   - **Example:** Fake anti-virus software that claims to detect issues and demands payment.
   - **Defense:** User training, anti-malware software, and vigilant monitoring.

4. **Doxware (Leakware):**

   - **Example:** Threatens to publish your data unless a ransom is paid.
   - **Defense:** Data encryption and access controls.

5. **Ransomware-as-a-Service (RaaS):**

   - **Example:** Cerber offers ransomware kits for sale, allowing less technical criminals to launch attacks.
   - **Defense:** Comprehensive security measures and continuous monitoring.

Practical Tip:

- Use an email filtering solution to scan and block malicious attachments and links. Train employees to recognize phishing attempts and report suspicious emails.

Risk Assessment

Identifying Vulnerabilities in Your Business

Conducting a thorough assessment of your IT infrastructure is the foundation of an effective cybersecurity strategy. Here are detailed steps to help you identify potential vulnerabilities:

1. **Software and Hardware Inventory:**

    - **Action:** Maintain a detailed inventory of all hardware and software, including versions and patch levels.
    - **Tool:** Use asset management tools like ManageEngine AssetExplorer or SolarWinds MSP.
    - **Tip:** Regularly audit your inventory to ensure all items are up to date and patched.

2. **Network Security:**

    - **Action:** Evaluate your network architecture and implement segmentation to isolate critical systems.
    - **Tool:** Employ network monitoring tools such as Wireshark or SolarWinds Network Performance Monitor.
    - **Tip:** Regularly update firewall rules and conduct penetration testing to identify weaknesses.

3. **Access Controls:**

    - **Action:** Implement role-based access control (RBAC) to ensure users only have access to necessary resources.
    - **Tool:** Use IAM (Identity and Access Management) solutions like Okta or Microsoft Azure AD.
    - **Tip:** Regularly review access rights and remove or adjust them as needed.

4. **Data Storage and Backup:**

    - **Action:** Ensure critical data is backed up regularly and stored securely, both on-site and off-site.
    - **Tool:** Utilize backup solutions like Veeam or Acronis.
    - **Tip:** Perform regular backup tests to verify data integrity and recovery processes.

Assessing Potential Impact

Understanding the potential impact of a ransomware attack can help prioritize security efforts. Here's how to conduct a detailed impact assessment:

1. **Financial Impact:**

   - **Action:** Calculate potential financial losses from operational downtime, ransom payments, and recovery costs.
   - **Tool:** Use risk management tools like FAIR (Factor Analysis of Information Risk) to quantify financial impact.
   - **Tip:** Consider both direct and indirect costs, including potential legal fees and loss of business.

2. **Operational Impact:**

   - **Action:** Identify critical business processes and the systems they depend on.
   - **Tool:** Use business impact analysis (BIA) tools to map out dependencies and critical paths.
   - **Tip:** Develop continuity plans for each critical process to minimize disruption.

3. **Legal and Regulatory Impact:**

   - **Action:** Understand the legal requirements for data protection and breach notification in your jurisdiction.
   - **Tool:** Refer to compliance management tools like ComplyScore or RSA Archer.
   - **Tip:** Maintain a clear record of compliance efforts and incident response plans.

Prioritizing Risks

With vulnerabilities identified and potential impacts assessed, prioritize your risks to address the most critical areas first:

1. **Risk Matrix:**

   - **Action:** Use a risk matrix to categorize risks based on likelihood and impact.
   - **Tool:** Create a matrix in Excel or use dedicated risk management software like LogicManager.
   - **Tip:** Regularly update your risk matrix as new threats emerge and business processes change.

2. **Mitigation Strategies:**

   - **Action:** Develop and implement strategies to mitigate prioritized risks, focusing on high-impact, high-likelihood scenarios.
   - **Tool:** Use project management tools like Asana or Trello to track mitigation efforts.
   - **Tip:** Assign clear ownership for each mitigation strategy and set realistic deadlines.

3. **Continuous Monitoring:**

   - **Action:** Implement continuous monitoring of your systems to detect and respond to threats in real-time.
   - **Tool:** Use SIEM (Security Information and Event Management) tools like Splunk or QRadar.
   - **Tip:** Establish a Security Operations Center (SOC) to centralize monitoring and incident response.

Preventative Measures

Regular Software Updates and Patching

Keeping all software and systems up-to-date is crucial in preventing ransomware attacks. Outdated software often contains vulnerabilities that attackers can exploit.

Specific Steps:

1. **Automate Updates:**

   - **Action:** Use automated patch management tools to ensure that all software is regularly updated.
   - **Tool:** Solutions like Microsoft WSUS, Ivanti, or Patch My PC can automate the update process.
   - **Tip:** Schedule updates during off-peak hours to minimize disruption.

2. **Patch Management Policy:**

   - **Action:** Develop and implement a patch management policy that outlines the process for identifying, testing, and deploying patches.
   - **Template:** Use resources from the SANS Institute or NIST to create your policy.

3. **Vulnerability Scanning:**

   - **Action:** Regularly scan your systems for vulnerabilities using automated tools.
   - **Tool:** Tools like Nessus, Qualys, or OpenVAS can identify vulnerabilities that need to be patched.
   - **Tip:** Conduct scans at least once a month and after significant system changes.

Employee Training and Awareness

Employees are often the first line of defense against ransomware. Educating them on how to recognize and avoid potential threats is essential.

Specific Steps:

1. **Regular Training Sessions:**

   - **Action:** Conduct regular cybersecurity training sessions for all employees.
   - **Tool:** Platforms like KnowBe4, SANS Security Awareness, or Wombat Security can provide interactive training modules.
   - **Tip:** Include phishing simulations to test and reinforce training effectiveness.

2. **Phishing Awareness:**

   - **Action:** Teach employees how to identify phishing emails and report them.
   - **Tool:** Use email filtering solutions like Proofpoint or Mimecast to help identify and block phishing attempts.
   - **Tip:** Encourage a culture of vigilance where employees feel comfortable reporting suspicious emails.

3. **Security Policies:**

   - **Action:** Develop and enforce security policies that cover acceptable use, password management, and incident reporting.
   - **Template:** Leverage templates from NIST or ISO 27001 to create comprehensive policies.

Implementing Strong Password Policies

Weak passwords can be easily compromised, leading to unauthorized access and potential ransomware attacks.

Specific Steps:

1. **Password Complexity:**

   - **Action:** Enforce strong password policies requiring a mix of upper and lower case letters, numbers, and special characters.
   - **Tool:** Use password management tools like LastPass, 1Password, or Dashlane to help employees manage their passwords securely.
   - **Tip:** Implement regular password change intervals (e.g., every 90 days).

2. **Multi-Factor Authentication (MFA):**

   - **Action:** Implement MFA for all critical systems and services.
   - **Tool:** Solutions like Google Authenticator, Microsoft Authenticator, or Duo Security can add an extra layer of security.
   - **Tip:** Make MFA mandatory for remote access and sensitive operations.

3. **Password Management:**

   - **Action:** Use enterprise password management solutions to enforce policies and track compliance.
   - **Tool:** Tools like Thycotic Secret Server or CyberArk can manage and secure passwords enterprise-wide.
   - **Tip:** Regularly review and update password policies to adapt to new threats.

Network Segmentation and Firewalls

Segmenting your network and using robust firewalls can limit the spread of ransomware within your organization.

Specific Steps:

1. **Network Segmentation:**

   - **Action:** Divide your network into smaller segments to isolate critical systems.
   - **Tool:** Use VLANs (Virtual Local Area Networks) and subnetting to create isolated segments.
   - **Tip:** Ensure sensitive data and critical systems are on separate segments from general user access.

2. **Firewall Configuration:**

   - **Action:** Configure firewalls to control and monitor traffic between network segments.
   - **Tool:** Use next-generation firewalls (NGFW) like Palo Alto Networks, Fortinet, or Cisco Firepower.
   - **Tip:** Regularly review and update firewall rules to block unnecessary traffic and potential threats.

3. **Intrusion Detection and Prevention:**

   - **Action:** Implement IDS/IPS to monitor network traffic and block malicious activities.
   - **Tool:** Solutions like Snort, Suricata, or Cisco Secure IDS can provide real-time threat detection and prevention.
   - **Tip:** Integrate IDS/IPS with your SIEM (Security Information and Event Management) for comprehensive monitoring.

Backup Strategies and Data Recovery Plans

Regular and reliable backups are essential to recovering from a ransomware attack without paying the ransom.

Specific Steps:

1. **Regular Backups:**

   - **Action:** Implement a regular backup schedule for all critical data.
   - **Tool:** Use backup solutions like Acronis, Veeam, or Carbonite to automate and manage backups.
   - **Tip:** Follow the 3-2-1 backup rule: three copies of your data, on two different media, with one copy off-site.

2. **Secure Backup Storage:**

   - **Action:** Store backups in a secure location, preferably offline or in a separate network segment.
   - **Tool:** Solutions like Iron Mountain for physical storage or cloud services like Amazon S3 for off-site backups.
   - **Tip:** Encrypt backups to protect against unauthorized access.

3. **Testing and Validation:**

   - **Action:** Regularly test your backups to ensure they can be restored effectively.
   - **Tool:** Use backup validation tools provided by your backup solution to verify data integrity.
   - **Tip:** Conduct regular disaster recovery drills to test your data recovery plans.

Technical Defenses

Anti-Virus and Anti-Malware Solutions

Implementing robust anti-virus and anti-malware solutions is essential for detecting and preventing ransomware and other malicious software.

Specific Steps:

1. **Selecting Anti-Virus Software:**

   - **Action:** Choose a reputable anti-virus solution with real-time scanning and heuristic analysis.
   - **Tool:** Solutions like Bitdefender, Norton, or Kaspersky provide comprehensive protection.
   - **Tip:** Ensure the software is regularly updated to protect against new threats.

2. **Deploying Anti-Malware Tools:**

   - **Action:** Use specialized anti-malware tools alongside your anti-virus software for layered protection.
   - **Tool:** Malwarebytes and HitmanPro are excellent options for detecting and removing malware.
   - **Tip:** Schedule regular scans during off-hours to minimize disruption.

3. **Centralized Management:**

   - **Action:** Implement centralized management for deploying and monitoring anti-virus and anti-malware solutions across all devices.
   - **Tool:** Solutions like Symantec Endpoint Protection Manager or McAfee ePolicy Orchestrator can help manage security policies and updates.
   - **Tip:** Regularly review security reports to identify and address vulnerabilities promptly.

Intrusion Detection and Prevention Systems

Intrusion Detection Systems (IDS) and Intrusion Prevention Systems (IPS) are critical for monitoring and blocking suspicious network activity.

Specific Steps:

1. **Implementing IDS/IPS:**

   - **Action:** Deploy IDS/IPS to monitor network traffic and detect anomalies.
   - **Tool:** Solutions like Snort, Suricata, or Cisco Secure IDS/IPS provide robust detection capabilities.
   - **Tip:** Regularly update IDS/IPS signatures to recognize new threats.

2. **Configuring Alerts:**

   - **Action:** Set up alerts to notify administrators of potential intrusions or suspicious activity.
   - **Tool:** Integrate IDS/IPS with SIEM tools like Splunk or QRadar for centralized alert management.
   - **Tip:** Create a response plan for handling alerts and mitigating threats quickly.

3. **Regular Audits:**

   - **Action:** Conduct regular audits of IDS/IPS configurations and logs to ensure they are functioning correctly.
   - **Tool:** Use audit tools provided by your IDS/IPS solution or third-party tools like Nessus for comprehensive assessments.
   - **Tip:** Schedule audits at least quarterly or after significant network changes.

Endpoint Protection

Comprehensive endpoint protection is crucial for securing all devices that connect to your network, including desktops, laptops, and mobile devices.

Specific Steps:

1. **Deploying Endpoint Protection Platforms (EPP):**

   - **Action:** Implement EPP solutions to provide multi-layered protection for endpoints.
   - **Tool:** Solutions like CrowdStrike Falcon, Symantec Endpoint Protection, or McAfee Endpoint Security offer robust protection.
   - **Tip:** Ensure that all endpoints are enrolled in the EPP and regularly updated.

2. **Device Control:**

   - **Action:** Use endpoint protection tools to control and monitor device usage, including USB drives and external storage.
   - **Tool:** Solutions like Symantec or Bitdefender GravityZone provide device control features.
   - **Tip:** Restrict the use of removable media to minimize the risk of introducing malware.

3. **Application Whitelisting:**

   - **Action:** Implement application whitelisting to allow only approved applications to run on endpoints.
   - **Tool:** Use tools like AppLocker (Windows) or Carbon Black to enforce whitelisting policies.
   - **Tip:** Regularly review and update the whitelist to accommodate necessary software changes.

Secure Email Gateways

Email is a common vector for ransomware attacks. Secure email gateways (SEG) help filter and block malicious emails before they reach end users.

Specific Steps:

1. **Deploying SEG Solutions:**

   - **Action:** Implement SEG solutions to scan and filter incoming and outgoing emails.
   - **Tool:** Solutions like Proofpoint, Mimecast, or Barracuda Email Security Gateway provide advanced email protection.
   - **Tip:** Enable advanced threat protection features like sandboxing to analyze suspicious attachments and links.

2. **Phishing and Spam Filtering:**

   - **Action:** Configure SEG to filter phishing emails and spam effectively.
   - **Tool:** Use built-in phishing and spam filtering capabilities of SEG solutions or supplement with additional tools like Microsoft Defender for Office 365.
   - **Tip:** Regularly update filtering rules and algorithms to adapt to new phishing techniques.

3. **Email Encryption:**

   - **Action:** Implement email encryption to protect sensitive information in transit.
   - **Tool:** Solutions like Zix, Virtru, or Symantec Email Security.cloud provide robust encryption capabilities.
   - **Tip:** Educate employees on when and how to use email encryption for sensitive communications.

Incident Response Plan

Steps to Take During an Attack

Having a well-defined incident response plan is crucial for minimizing damage and recovering quickly from a ransomware attack. Here's a detailed guide on what to do during an attack:

1. **Isolate the Infection:**

   - **Action:** Immediately disconnect infected systems from the network to prevent the ransomware from spreading.
   - **Tool:** Use network management tools to isolate devices, or physically disconnect Ethernet cables and disable Wi-Fi.
   - **Tip:** Train staff to recognize signs of an attack and empower them to isolate systems without waiting for IT.

2. **Assess the Scope of the Attack:**

   - **Action:** Identify which systems and data have been affected.
   - **Tool:** Use forensic analysis tools like EnCase or FTK Imager to assess the extent of the damage.
   - **Tip:** Document the ransomware variant and attack vector for future reference.

3. **Notify Relevant Parties:**

   - **Action:** Inform your IT team, management, and any affected employees immediately.
   - **Tool:** Use communication tools like Slack, Microsoft Teams, or a dedicated incident response platform.
   - **Tip:** Have a predefined communication plan in place to ensure timely and effective information sharing.

4. **Preserve Evidence:**

   - **Action:** Avoid making changes to infected systems to preserve evidence for forensic analysis.
   - **Tool:** Use write blockers and forensic imaging tools to capture system snapshots.
   - **Tip:** Keep detailed logs of all actions taken during the incident response.

Communication Strategies

Effective communication is essential during a ransomware attack to manage the situation and maintain trust with stakeholders.

1. **Internal Communication:**

   - **Action:** Keep employees informed about the incident and provide clear instructions on what to do.
   - **Tool:** Use internal communication tools like email, intranet, or messaging apps.
   - **Tip:** Ensure communication is clear, concise, and avoids technical jargon.

2. **External Communication:**

   - **Action:** Notify customers, partners, and stakeholders if their data has been compromised.
   - **Tool:** Use email templates and communication platforms to reach external parties quickly.
   - **Tip:** Be transparent about the steps being taken to address the issue and offer support where needed.

3. **Media and Public Relations:**

   - **Action:** Prepare a public statement to address any media inquiries.
   - **Tool:** Use PR tools and services to manage media relations.
   - **Tip:** Ensure consistency in messaging and provide regular updates as the situation evolves.

Legal and Regulatory Considerations

Ransomware attacks can have significant legal and regulatory implications. Here's how to navigate these challenges:

1. **Reporting Requirements:**

    - **Action:** Determine if you need to report the incident to regulatory authorities.
    - **Tool:** Use compliance management tools to track reporting requirements.
    - **Tip:** Familiarize yourself with data breach notification laws in your jurisdiction.

2. **Data Protection Laws:**

    - **Action:** Ensure compliance with data protection laws such as GDPR or CCPA.
    - **Tool:** Use data privacy management solutions to help with compliance.
    - **Tip:** Document all steps taken to address the incident and protect affected data.

3. **Legal Advice:**

    - **Action:** Consult with legal counsel to understand your rights and responsibilities.
    - **Tool:** Work with specialized cybersecurity legal firms for expert advice.
    - **Tip:** Have a pre-established relationship with legal counsel to expedite the consultation process during an incident.

Working with Law Enforcement

Involving law enforcement can provide valuable support and increase the chances of tracking down the attackers.

1. **Report the Incident:**

   - **Action:** Contact local law enforcement or cybercrime units to report the attack.
   - **Tool:** Use contact information provided by organizations like the FBI's Internet Crime Complaint Center (IC3).
   - **Tip:** Provide detailed information and evidence to assist the investigation.

2. **Cooperate Fully:**

   - **Action:** Work closely with law enforcement throughout the investigation.
   - **Tool:** Maintain open lines of communication and provide updates as needed.
   - **Tip:** Follow law enforcement advice on handling the ransom demand and other aspects of the incident.

3. **Consider Cyber Insurance:**

   - **Action:** If you have cyber insurance, notify your provider about the attack.
   - **Tool:** Use your insurer's incident response resources and support.
   - **Tip:** Understand your policy coverage and the claims process in advance.

Case Studies

Example 1: Small Retail Business

Background: A small retail business with multiple locations experienced a ransomware attack that encrypted their point-of-sale (POS) systems.

Incident: The ransomware entered the system through a phishing email opened by an employee. Within minutes, all POS systems were locked, and a ransom note demanded $10,000 in Bitcoin for the decryption key.

Response:

1. **Isolation:** The IT team quickly disconnected all infected systems from the network.
2. **Assessment:** They identified the ransomware strain as a variant of CryptoLocker.
3. **Backup Restoration:** The business had regular backups of their POS data. They wiped the infected systems and restored data from the latest backup.
4. **Employee Training:** Post-incident, the business implemented mandatory cybersecurity training for all employees to prevent future incidents.

Outcome: The business did not pay the ransom. By having a solid backup strategy and swift incident response, they minimized downtime and financial loss. They also updated their email filtering system to prevent similar attacks.

Lessons Learned:

- Importance of regular backups and quick restoration procedures.
- Necessity of employee training and awareness programs.
- Enhanced email filtering and security measures are critical.

Example 2: Professional Services Firm

Background: A professional services firm specializing in legal and financial consulting was targeted by a sophisticated ransomware attack.

Incident: The attackers exploited a vulnerability in outdated software. The ransomware spread quickly, encrypting sensitive client documents and financial records.

Response:

1. **Forensic Analysis:** The firm hired cybersecurity experts to conduct a forensic analysis and identify the entry point.
2. **Communication:** They informed clients about the breach and assured them that steps were being taken to mitigate the impact.
3. **Payment:** Due to the sensitive nature of the encrypted data and the potential reputational damage, the firm decided to pay the ransom. They negotiated the amount down to $50,000.
4. **System Overhaul:** Post-attack, the firm updated all software, implemented multi-factor authentication, and strengthened their overall cybersecurity posture.

Outcome: While paying the ransom was a difficult decision, the firm prioritized client trust and data integrity. They have since taken extensive measures to prevent future attacks, including hiring a full-time cybersecurity specialist.

Lessons Learned:

- Critical need for keeping software and systems updated.
- Importance of client communication and transparency.
- Strategic decision-making during crises, even if it involves difficult choices.

Example 3: Nonprofit Organization

Background: A nonprofit organization that provides educational resources to underprivileged communities fell victim to a ransomware attack.

Incident: The ransomware was introduced through a malicious website link. It quickly encrypted the organization's database of donor information and educational materials.

Response:

1. **Incident Response Plan:** The organization followed their pre-established incident response plan, which included isolating the affected systems and notifying stakeholders.
2. **Law Enforcement:** They reported the incident to local law enforcement and sought assistance from cybersecurity professionals.
3. **Community Support:** The nonprofit reached out to their community for support. Volunteers helped rebuild systems and restore data from partial backups.

Outcome: The nonprofit did not pay the ransom. Although they lost some data, the community rallied to support their recovery efforts. The incident highlighted the importance of cybersecurity even for organizations with limited resources.

Lessons Learned:

- Value of a pre-established incident response plan.
- Importance of community and volunteer support in recovery efforts.
- Awareness and training can significantly mitigate risks, even with limited resources.

Resources and Tools

Recommended Software and Services

To strengthen your cybersecurity defenses against ransomware, consider utilizing these specific software and services:

1. **Anti-Virus and Anti-Malware Solutions:**

   - **Bitdefender:** Provides comprehensive protection with features like advanced threat defense, ransomware remediation, and network threat prevention.
     - **Website:** bitdefender.com
   - **Norton 360:** Offers real-time threat protection, a secure VPN, and dark web monitoring, along with robust anti-virus and anti-malware features.
     - **Website:** norton.com
   - **Malwarebytes:** Specializes in malware and ransomware protection with capabilities to detect and remove a wide range of threats.
     - **Website:** malwarebytes.com

2. **Backup Solutions:**

   - **Acronis True Image:** Provides reliable backup and recovery solutions with integrated ransomware protection.
     - **Website:** acronis.com
   - **Carbonite:** Offers automatic cloud backup services designed for small businesses, ensuring data is secure and recoverable.
     - **Website:** carbonite.com
   - **Veeam Backup & Replication:** Delivers advanced backup and replication solutions suitable for various environments, including virtual and physical servers.
     - **Website:** veeam.com

3. **Network Security:**

   - **Cisco Meraki:** Provides comprehensive security solutions, including firewall, intrusion detection, and secure Wi-Fi.
     - **Website:** meraki.cisco.com
   - **SonicWall:** Offers next-generation firewalls and secure mobile access solutions tailored for small to medium-sized businesses.
     - **Website:** sonicwall.com
   - **Ubiquiti Networks:** Delivers robust network security hardware with easy-to-use management software.
     - **Website:** ui.com

4. **Endpoint Protection:**

- **Symantec Endpoint Protection:** Combines anti-malware, intrusion prevention, and firewall features to protect endpoints from a wide range of threats.
    - **Website:** broadcom.com
- **CrowdStrike Falcon:** Provides cloud-delivered endpoint protection with AI-powered threat detection and response.
    - **Website:** crowdstrike.com
- **Kaspersky Endpoint Security:** Offers multi-layered protection against ransomware and other cyber threats, with features like encryption and application control.
    - **Website:** kaspersky.com

5. **Secure Email Gateways:**

- **Proofpoint:** Protects against email-based threats such as phishing, malware, and ransomware with advanced threat protection.
    - **Website:** proofpoint.com
- **Mimecast:** Provides email security, archiving, and continuity services to protect business communications.
    - **Website:** mimecast.com
- **Barracuda Email Security Gateway:** Delivers advanced email threat protection with features like spam filtering and data loss prevention.
    - **Website:** barracuda.com

Useful Websites and Further Reading

Staying informed about the latest developments in ransomware and cybersecurity is crucial. Here are some valuable resources:

1. **Cybersecurity and Infrastructure Security Agency (CISA):** Provides comprehensive resources, guidelines, and alerts on cybersecurity threats and best practices.
   - **Website:** cisa.gov
2. **National Institute of Standards and Technology (NIST):** Offers cybersecurity frameworks, guidelines, and standards to help organizations improve their security posture.
   - **Website:** nist.gov
3. **Krebs on Security:** A blog by cybersecurity expert Brian Krebs that covers the latest news and insights on cyber threats, including ransomware.
   - **Website:** krebsonsecurity.com
4. **SANS Institute:** Provides cybersecurity training, research, and certification programs, along with valuable resources on ransomware and other threats.
   - **Website:** sans.org
5. **Bleeping Computer:** Offers news, guides, and forums on a wide range of cybersecurity topics, including ransomware.
   - **Website:** bleepingcomputer.com

Templates for Policies and Procedures

Implementing standardized policies and procedures enhances your cybersecurity measures and preparedness. Below are some templates to help you get started:

1. **Incident Response Plan Template:**

   - **Action:** Outline the steps to take in the event of a ransomware attack, including communication strategies and legal considerations.
   - **Resource:** SANS Incident Handler's Handbook

2. **Data Backup Policy Template:**

   - **Action:** Define procedures for regular data backups, including frequency, storage locations, and recovery processes.
   - **Resource:** TechRepublic Data Backup Policy

3. **Password Policy Template:**

   - **Action:** Establish guidelines for creating and maintaining strong passwords, including complexity requirements and expiration policies.
   - **Resource:** NIST Password Policy Guidelines

4. **Employee Training Program Template:**

   - **Action:** Develop a training program to educate employees on cybersecurity best practices, including phishing awareness and safe browsing.
   - **Resource:** Cybersecurity Training Resources by CISA

Conclusion

The Ongoing Battle Against Ransomware

Ransomware is a constant and evolving threat that can cause serious problems for businesses. While attackers keep finding new ways to break in, you can stay safe by being careful and prepared. This book has given you the knowledge and tools to protect your business, respond to attacks, and recover quickly.

Key Points:

- Ransomware attacks can lead to big financial losses, stop your business operations, and damage your reputation.
- Having a strong security plan, training your employees, and being ready for an attack are important parts of your defense.
- Keep watching for new threats and update your security measures regularly.

Staying Vigilant and Prepared

The key to staying safe from ransomware is being prepared and careful. Regularly check and update your security measures, train your employees, and test your response plans. By taking a proactive approach to cybersecurity, you can protect your business, your customers, and your reputation from ransomware.

Action Steps:

1. **Regular Assessments:** Check your systems often to find and fix any weaknesses.
2. **Employee Training:** Keep training your employees so they know the latest threats and best practices.
3. **Incident Response Testing:** Test your response plans regularly to make sure they work.
4. **Continuous Improvement:** Stay informed about new threats and keep improving your defenses.

Appendices

Glossary of Terms

- **Anti-Malware:** Software that finds and stops malicious software.
- **Backup:** A copy of your data stored separately to protect against loss.
- **Crypto Ransomware:** Ransomware that encrypts files and demands payment for the key.
- **Endpoint:** Any device that connects to a network, like a computer or phone.
- **Firewall:** A device or software that monitors and controls network traffic.
- **Intrusion Detection System (IDS):** A system that watches for suspicious activity on a network
- **Intrusion Prevention System (IPS):** A system that blocks malicious activity on a network.
- **Multi-Factor Authentication (MFA):** A security process that requires two or more ways to verify your identity.
- **Phishing:** A type of attack where fake emails or websites trick people into giving sensitive information.
- **Ransomware:** Malicious software that locks your data and demands payment to unlock it.
- **Secure Email Gateway (SEG):** A security solution that filters email to block threats like phishing and malware.

Sample Incident Response Plan

1. **Preparation:**

   - Set up a response team and define roles.
   - Write down your incident response policy.
   - Train and practice regularly.

2. **Identification:**

   - Watch for signs of a ransomware attack.
   - Confirm and classify the incident.

3. **Containment:**

   - Isolate affected systems to stop the ransomware from spreading.
   - Use short-term measures to contain the attack.

4. **Eradication:**

   - Find and remove the ransomware.
   - Update systems to prevent another attack.

5. **Recovery:**

   - Restore data from backups.
   - Check that systems are working and secure.

6. **Lessons Learned:**

   - Review the incident and improve your plan.
   - Update policies and procedures based on what you learned.

Checklist for Ransomware Preparedness

- Update and patch software regularly.
- Train employees on cybersecurity best practices.
- Enforce strong password policies and use multi-factor authentication.
- Segment your network and use strong firewalls.
- Back up data regularly and test your backups.
- Use anti-virus and anti-malware solutions.
- Filter email threats with a secure email gateway.
- Have a documented incident response plan.
- Regularly review and update your security measures.

About the author: j. p. ames

Mr. Ames is a four-decade computer scientist who has traveled the world for his work. Living near New York City for more than 30 years, he speaks Spanish and enjoys writing books on a diverse range of topics including romance, science fiction, history, pop culture, artificial intelligence, quantum physics, spy satellites, classic television and travel photography. Mr. Ames is an FCC licensee, also certified in virtualization and advanced firewalls. His hobbies include collecting coins, fluorescent and phosphorescent minerals, Amateur radio and enjoying time outdoors with his wife and children as well as studying historic computer operating systems. His business, Cartoon Renewal Studios, employs Artificial Intelligence to restore, upscale and colorize historic films and cartoons.

www.ingramcontent.com/pod-product-compliance
Lightning Source LLC
LaVergne TN
LVHW051650050326
832903LV00034B/4785